ALL LONDON

Text by ERIC RESTALL

Photographs, lay-out and reproduction, entirely designed and created by the Technical Department of EDITORIAL ESCUDO DE ORO, S.A.

Rights of total or partial reproduction and translation reserved.

5th Edition, April 1982

I.S.B.N. 84-378-0268-7

| English | 84-378-0304-7 |
| German | 84-378-0305-5 |

Dep. Legal B. 4955-XXV

DISTRIBUTOR: FISA (GREAT BRITAIN) Ltd. 25, Denmark Street
LONDON WC 2

Impreso en España - Printed in Spain
F.I.S.A. Palaudarias, 26 - Barcelona-4

One of the earliest paintings of London, circa *1500*.

King John's *Charter, 1215.*

The *Great Fire* of London, *1666.*

THE CITY

Modern London is a hybrid creature formed from the ancient cities of London and Westminster evolving over the centuries into what is today a sprawling metropolis comprising some 8,000,000 inhabitants in an area of about 610 square miles. But it is in the City that we must look for the origins of the London we know today. London, the greatest city in the world, is at least two thousand years old and was settled long before the first Roman invasion. Over the centuries the City has jealously guarded its independence which has been recognised by a series of royal charters. William the Conqueror acknowledged the City's special privileges as did King John in a Charter dated 9 May 1215 which confirmed the right to choose a Mayor by annual election.

The medieval face of London was dramatically changed by the Great Fire which broke out on 2 September 1666 in Pudding Lane, less than a year after the Great Plague that in a single week had claimed over 12,000 lives. During a period of four days 13,000 houses and over 80 churches were destroyed. The Great Fire consumed many of the fine livery halls of the City Companies, the Royal Exchange, the Guildhall (only the walls and crypt escaped) the Fish Market at Billingsgate, Fleet and Bridewell Prisons, Ludgate, Aldersgate and Newgate (three of the ancient City gates), and St. Paul's Cathedral. Miraculously only a few lives were lost but the Fire destroyed over three-quarters of the City and along with it priceless records and fine examples of medieval architecture both civil and religious. *The Monument* was designed by Sir Christopher Wren, in collaboration with Robert Hooke, and erected in 1677 to commemorate the Great Fire. The Portland stone fluted column is 202 feet high, surmounted by a platform and topped by a gilded flaming urn. The height is reputed to be the exact distance from where the fire started. Three hundred and eleven steps inside the pillar lead to a balcony from which there is a marvellous view of London. "The Fat Boy", a small gilded wooden figure situated high up on a wall in Cock Lane, Giltspur Street, Smithfield, marks the farthest limit of the Fire.

The Central Criminal Court, more popularly known as the Old Bailey, was built in 1907 near the site of the infamous Newgate which was London's main prison from the thirteenth century. Contrary to popular belief the figure of Justice, topping the copper dome, holding a sword in one hand and the scales of justice in the other, is *not* blindfolded.

Doctor Johnson's House, Gough Square, off Fleet Street is a delightful example of Queen Anne domestic architecture. The Doctor lived here between 1748-1759 and compiled his famous *Dictionary* in the attic at the top of the house with the help of six assistants. The house contains many Johnson relics including his armchair, let-

Temple Bar (left), *The Guildhall* (bottom), *and* (top)
The Fat Boy.

ters and prints of friends — Mrs. Thrale, Fanny Burney, Oliver Goldsmith, David Garrick, Sir Joshua Reynolds and his biographer James Boswell. The nearby *Cheshire Cheese* in Wine Court Lodge was a popular eating-place for Johnson and his contemporaries as it is today for the tourist. Johnson might well have been thinking of this seventeenth-century tavern when he said "There is nothing which has yet been contrived by man, by which so much happiness is produced as by a good tavern or inn".

Within this one square mile of concentrated history and amid the continuously changing face of the City is the world's financial and commercial centre. *Lloyd's,* typical of so many City institutions, was founded in a coffee shop at the end of the seventeenth century. Originally concerned exclusively with maritime insurance, today its syndicates of some 5,000 members underwrite an astonishing range of world-wide risks. In the centre of the Underwriting Room hangs the Lutine Bell which is rung to mark an important announcement — one stroke means bad news and two good news. The bell came from the frigate *La Lutine* which sank in 1799 with a cargo of gold which was insured by Lloyd's.

The Guildhall, or the Hall of Guilds, is the seat of City government for here is where the Court of Common Council meets. The election of the Lord Mayor and Sheriffs and state banquets take place in the Great Hall with much pomp and pageantry. In this same hall the unfortunate Lady Jane Grey (the nine-day Queen) and her husband were tried and sentenced to death in 1553. The two giant carved figures at the far end of the Great Hall are Gog and Magog, modern versions of the originals which were destroyed in the Great Fire. The present building dates from the beginning of the fifteenth century though it suffered much damage during the Great Fire and again in the Second World War.

The Bank of England (left) *and* (centre) *the Royal Exchange.*

The Stock Exchange and (below) *the Underwriting Room at Lloyd's.*

The Old Bailey (top) and (bottom) the Griffin marking the City boundary on the Embankment.

The Mansion House is the official residence of the Lord Mayor of London. Behind the Corinthian portico are many sumptuous apartments, the Court of Justice with cells below, and the Egyptian Hall used for state banquets.

Since 1970 the *Stock Exchange* has been housed in a new twenty-six storeyed complex in Old Broad Street. Visitors can watch this great financial institution in action from a gallery overlooking the "floor of the house". "My word is my bond" *(Dictum Meum Pactum)* is the motto of the Stock Exchange and today even among the sophisticated computer gadgetry verbal transactions are the basic form of business.

The Bank of England was founded in 1694 largely to finance the French wars during the reign of William and Mary. Within the vaults of "the Old Lady of Threadneedle Street" are kept the nation's gold reserves. The Bank was an independent company up to 1946 when it was nationalised and control passed to the Treasury.

The Royal Exchange was first founded about 1565 by that great financier, Sir Thomas Gresham, for "merchants to assemble in", but this building was destroyed in the Great Fire of London (1666) and its successor suffered a similar fate in 1838. The present building dates from 1844 but no business has been conducted from it since 1939. The equestrian statue of the Duke of Wellington is noted for its absence of stirrups.

The Temple of Mithras. During the preparation of the site for Bucklersbury House in 1954 the Roman Temple of Mithras was revealed. Subsequent excavations proved this to be a unique discovery; a pagan temple, dedicated to the Persian Sun-god. The Temple was later reconstructed only a short way from its original site and the relics are currently displayed in the new Museum of London in the Barbican.

London Stone was rescued from the ruins of St. Swithin's Church bombed in the last War, and set in the wall of the office building which stands on the same site. This stone is thought to be a Roman milestone from which distances were measured along the whole chain of Roman roads radiating from the City all over the country.

The Barbican is an imaginative development scheme in the northern part of the City covering an area of some thirty-five acres which had been devastated during the last War. It comprises multi-storey blocks of offices and some of the highest blocks of flats in Europe, shops, taverns, restaurants, an Arts Centre and a new Museum of London. A brave attempt by the planning authorities to provide a self-contained community with residential accommodation for some 6,500 people to live near the heart of the City.

THE TOWER OF LONDON

The approach to the Tower is by way of Tower Hill, the site of so many public executions in the past, but where today the public are more peacefully entertained by politicians, preachers, and "buskers".

There is more of London's history in the Tower than anywhere else. It is the oldest surviving building in London, dating from the Norman Conquest, and even before that the site had been used by the Romans, and later by the Saxons as a fortress.

From the eleventh century onwards the Tower has served many purposes — always a fortress but, at various periods of history, also as a royal palace (King Charles II was the last king to stay here and before him, King Henry III); a prison (the long list of unfortunate inmates includes Kings, Queens, Princes and Nobles); a treasury; a mint until 1810; an arsenal; the first royal observatory in the reign of King Charles II; and for three hundred years there was a royal zoo which was moved to Regent's Park in the 1830's.

The oldest part is the White Tower built as a fortress and family residence by William the Conqueror in 1078. The name is said to have originated in the reign of King Henry III who ordered the Tower to be whitewashed. Today the White Tower houses a unique collection of arms and armour and instruments of torture. The Chapel of St. John, on the first floor, is one of the finest surviving specimens of pure Norman architecture — a wonderful combination of immense strength with an impressive simplicity of line. Apart from the windows, which were enlarged by Sir Christopher Wren, the chapel is virtually in its original state. The Chapel has a long recorded history as it was within these walls that the Archbishop of Canterbury and the Chancellor were seized in 1381 during the Peasants' Revolt and taken to be murdered on Tower Hill; King Henry VI's body lay here after his murder in 1471; Mary Tudor went through a form of marriage by proxy to Philip, King of Spain; Lady Jane Grey (the nineday Queen) prayed here before her execution in 1553. Candidates for the Order of the Bath, the second oldest Order of Knighthood, kept their vigil through the night at its altar, and on the following morning received the accolade of Knighthood from the Monarch. This ceremony dates from 1399 and continued until the coronation of King Charles II.

Successive sovereigns were responsible for the many additional buildings that comprise the complex we see today. The inner defensive wall and its thirteen towers were added in the reign of King Henry III (1216 — 1272)

whilst King Edward I (1272 — 1307) was responsible for the construction of the outer defences, Traitors' Gate, the completion of the Moat (drained in 1843) and the Middle Tower. Legge's Mount and Brass Mount, two bastions on the outer wall, were built in the reign of King Henry VIII. The Tower has always been under the direct control of the Sovereign who appoints a Constable as her representative. Originally this appointment was for life but since 1938 the term of office has been five years. The actual day-to-day administration is in the hands of a resident Governor, assisted by the Yeoman Warders, more popularly known as Beefeaters. Their splendid State Dress, originating from 1552, is reserved for ceremonial duty and guarding royalty during their visits to the City of London. They are more usually seen in their informal blue uniforms, which were approved by Queen Victoria in 1858. The unofficial custodians of the Tower however are the Ravens, a part of the establishment whose presence, according to legend, is necessary to prevent disaster coming to the Tower.

Traitors' Gate is now seen as an enormous arch below the outer walls, with its portcullis, through which, when this was the main approach from the river, shackled prisoners passed on their final journey.

The delightful Tower Green, where so many visitors today pose for photographs, was not always so pleasant. Described by Macaulay (1800-1859) as "no sadder spot on earth", this was the site of the scaffold where the less common prisoners met their end. Here perished two of King Henry VIII's wives, Anne Boleyn and Catherine Howard. Lady Jane Grey and the Earl of Essex were also executed here.

It was in the Bloody Tower that King Richard III is alleged to have murdered his two young nephews, "the little Princes", in 1483. Sir Walter Raleigh after being imprisoned here for thirteen years was beheaded at Westminster in 1618.

The present Chapel Royal of St. Peter ad Vincula was built by King Henry VIII (1509-1547) but its origins date back to the beginning of the twelfth century. Here are buried the remains of Queen Anne Boleyn (1536), Queen Catherine Howard (1542), The Dukes of Northumberland (1553), Somerset (1551) and Monmouth (1685), Lady Jane Grey and her husband, Lord Guildford Dudley (1554), Robert Devereux, Earl of Essex (1601) as well as many others of rank and fame. The organ, originally in the Palace of Westminster, is the oldest remaining in the City of London, dating from 1676. The Chapel is hung with regimental colours and contains many monuments and tombs of historic interest.

The Crown Jewels had for many years been kept in the

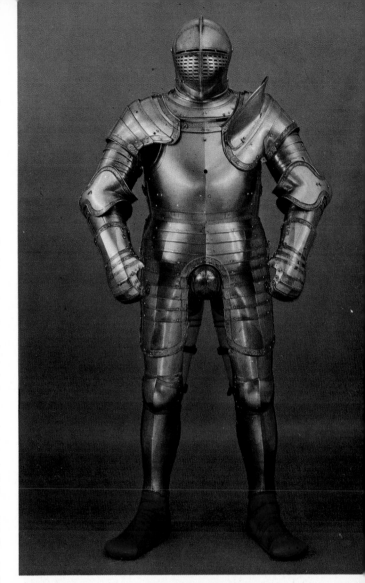

Armour made for King Henry VIII, circa *1540*
(top right) *and* (bottom) *the block and axe.*

Wakefield Tower but since 1967 have been housed in a specially constructed strongroom below the Waterloo Barracks. Here is probably the world's largest and most valuable collection of jewels and gold plate, comprising the Coronation Regalia, most of which, due to the hatred of everything royal by Oliver Cromwell, dates from 1660. Three notable exceptions are Queen Elizabeth I's salt cellar, which is the oldest of the gold plate, the twelfth-century anointing spoon, and the Ampulla, the age of which cannot be determined for certain, although it is believed to have been used at the Coronation of Henry IV in 1399.

The original Crown of England (St. Edward's Crown) was one of the many treasures destroyed by Cromwell, and the Crown on display today is a copy made for the coronation of King Charles II. The Imperial State Crown, worn by the Monarch at the opening of Parliament and other state occasions, was made by command of Queen Victoria and first used at her coronation in 1838. This is possibly the most valuable crown in the world, containing many precious diamonds, rubies, sapphires and emeralds. Among the many famous and historic stones in this crown are the Stuart Sapphire, the Black Prince's Ruby and the second Star of Africa. The Queen Mother's Crown, made for the coronation of Her Majesty Queen Elizabeth in 1937, contains the famous and beautiful Koh-i-noor diamond, which, according to legend, brings misfortune to male owners. This magnificent diamond is the large stone at the centre point of the cross.

Among the splendid objects of royal regalia, the Sovereign's Orb and Sceptre are the most striking and valuable, containing the Great Star of Africa which weighs 530 carats and is the largest cut diamond in the world. Of the many swords displayed, the jewelled Great Sword of State, dating from the late seventeenth century, is undoubtedly the most spectacular. Its scabbard is decorated with diamonds, emeralds, and rubies, in designs forming the Rose of England, the Thistle of Scotland and the Shamrock of Ireland.

Every evening, in accordance with ancient custom, the Tower is ritually secured by the Ceremony of the Keys. All the main gates are formally closed and locked during a ceremony which concludes with a challenge by the guard on duty at the Bloody Tower who says, "Halt, who comes here?" The Chief Warder answers, "The Keys". Sentry: "Whose Keys?". Chief Warder: "Queen Elizabeth's Keys". Sentry: "Advance Queen Elizabeth's Keys. All's well". The Keys are then taken to the Queen's House for handing into the custody of the Governor and the ceremony concludes with the bugler sounding the "Last Post".

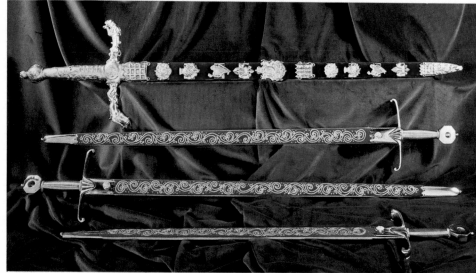

The Ampulla and Annointing Spoon
(top left).
Sovereign's Orb and Sceptre (top right).

The Coronation Rings (centre left).
The Swords of State (centre right).

Queen Elizabeth, the Queen Mother's
Crown (bottom left).
The Imperial State Crown (bottom right).

St. Edward's Crown (facing page).

ST PAUL'S CATHEDRAL

Sir Christopher Wren's masterpiece stands on a site occupied by several predecessors, the last of which perished in the Great Fire of London in 1666. The building of the present Cathedral commenced in 1675 and the last stone was laid in 1710. Acclaimed by many authorities as one of the most beautiful Renaissance buildings in the world, its dome is only surpassed in size by St Peter's in Rome.

The inner dome is decorated by paintings by Sir James Thornhill depicting the life of St Paul, and above it there is the larger outer dome constructed of wood covered with lead. Visitors are strongly recommended to make the ascent to the Whispering Gallery in order to experience the acoustic phenomenon from which it gets its name, and thence on to the exterior Stone Gallery from where the whole of London is visible. Those with sufficient stamina may continue higher yet, up to the Golden Gallery and then finally into the Golden Ball itself on which the Golden Cross dominates the City of London.

The magnificent interior of the Cathedral contains many fine paintings, sculptures, monuments and works of art, foremost of which are the original choir stalls carved by Wren's contemporary, Grinling Gibbons, the fine wrought-iron work by Tijou, another contemporary, the new High Altar based on Wren's own design and dedicated to Commonwealth troops who died in the Second World War, and the American Memorial Chapel in the apse behind the Altar. One object which miraculously survived the Great Fire is the macabre statue of John Donne the poet. Also here are Holman Hunt's copy of his famous painting *The Light of the World,* memorials to artists Turner, Reynolds, Van Dyck, Millais, Constable, and Blake; soldiers Sir John Moore, General Gordon, Lord Kitchener and the mighty sarcophagus of the Duke of Wellington. Lord Nelson's remains are interred in a black marble sarcophagus made originally for Henry VIII, whilst those of the master architect lie in the crypt with the simple inscription *Si Monumentum requiris circumspice* (If you seek a memorial, look around you).

The nave, looking east. ▷

Sir Christopher Wren, architect of St. Paul's Cathedral,
a portrait by Closterman, circa 1695.

THE LIGHT
OF THE WORLD

BEHOLD I STAND AT THE DOOR AND KNOCK IF ANY MAN
HEAR MY VOICE AND OPEN THE DOOR I WILL COME
IN TO HIM AND WILL SVP WITH HIM AND HE WITH ME.

Choir-stalls, carving by Grinling Gibbons.

Holman Hunt's The Light of the World.

WESTMINSTER ABBEY

One of the finest examples of Early English Gothic architecture, founded by Edward the Confessor in 1065 on the site of a church which had been built 500 years earlier. "The Abbey", as it is affectionately known to the English, but more properly the Collegiate Church of St. Peter in Westminster, was mostly built in the thirteenth century during the reign of Henry III.

Entering by the west door the gaze is directed upwards to the vaulted ceiling, then along the great nave lit by the aisle and clerestory windows above. Despite the advice often given to ignore the clutter of memorials, these testimonials to the great dead are the very stuff of which history is made. This is where all the English monarchs have been crowned for over 600 years and many of them subsequently buried, their magnificent tombs surrounded by a proliferation of commoners — prime ministers, artists, physicians, poets, actors, authors, soldiers and sailors, politicians. Holding pride of place is the tomb of the Unknown Warrior, just inside the west door, commemorating the nation's dead of all ranks and Services, nearly a million who perished in the First World War.

Among the famous persons buried or commemorated here are Queen Elizabeth I; the tragic Mary, Queen of Scots, beheaded in 1587 by order of her cousin and reburied in the Abbey 25 years later by command of her son, King James I; King George II (the last sovereign to be buried in the Abbey); *Soldiers:* Field Marshal Allenby, General Gordon, Lord Baden-Powell; *Scientists:* Sir Isaac Newton, Darwin; *Writers:* Thackeray, Ruskin, Goldsmith, Burns, Wordsworth, Browning, Milton, Chaucer, Ben Jonson (incorrectly spelt Johnson), Samuel Johnson, Dickens, Shakespeare; *Musicians:* Handel, Purcell; *Statesmen:* Disraeli, Chamberlain, Gladstone, Palmerston, Fox, Pitt; *Actors:* Irving, Garrick; and *Painter:* Kneller (the only painter so honoured), and many, many others.

The Abbey's founder is buried in the Chapel of Edward the Confessor where his time-worn tomb was for hundreds of years a place of pilgrimage. The tomb's outer covering of gold and precious stones was stripped during the Reformation as was the original silver head from the nearby effigy of Henry V.

The Chapel also contains the tombs of Henry VIII, Edward I and his wife Eleanor of Castile, Edward III, Richard II (his portrait, the earliest contemporary painting of an English King, hangs in the nave by the west door), Phillippa of Hainault and Anne of Bohemia.

The most sumptuous single addition to the Abbey is unquestionably Henry VII's Chapel at the eastern end, described by a contemporary antiquary, John Leland, as one of the wonders of the world. Henry was buried here in 1509 alongside his Queen, Elizabeth of York, who six years before had died in childbirth. The delicate lacework

The nave, looking west.

The best known
view of the
Abbey: the
West Door

King Henry
VIII's Chapel.

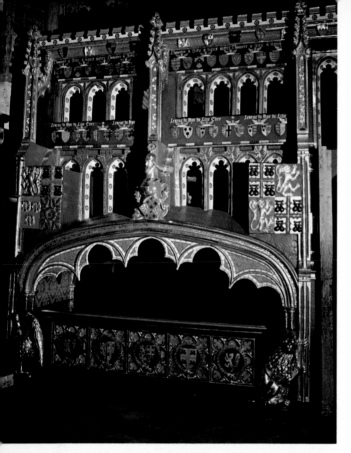

tracery of the fan-vaulted ceiling is unparalleled in the whole of England.

The octagonal Chapter House, dating from the mid-thirteenth century, has seen endless restorations, though much of the original fabric remains along with the floor tiles which surprisingly have survived to this day. On the plain stone benches around the walls sat the medieval monks at their business. For over one hundred and fifty years the Chapter House was used as Parliament House, until 1547 when King Edward VI allowed the House of Commons to meet in St. Stephens Chapel in the old Palace of Westminster. Thereafter the Chapter House fell into disuse until 1860 when major restorations were carried out by Sir George Gilbert Scott. The Coronation Chair is situated between the High Altar and the Chapel of Edward the Confessor. The oak chair which was built by order of Edward In 1300 to contain the legendary Stone of Scone, captured four years earlier in Scotland, has been used for every Coronation since 1308.

Visitors would also be well advised to see the Museum and the adjacent Chapel of the Pyx which in ancient times was used as the Royal Treasury. Here was kept the Pyx, a box containing standard coins of the realm against which current gold and silver coins were tested each year for weight and purity of metal.

The Coronation Chair and the Stone of Scone.

Decorated monuments: Lord and Baroness Bourchier
(top left), *Lady Burghley and her daughter, Anne, Countess
of Oxford* (top right).

THE HOUSES OF PARLIAMENT

Dominating the eastern extremity of the complex of buildings known as the Houses of Parliament, but more correctly the Palace of Westminster, is the 320 foot high tower housing the Palace clock. Famed throughout the world as Big Ben (actually the name of the bell), it was reputedly so called after Sir Benjamin Hall, the burly Commissioner of Works when it was installed in 1858. A light above the clock signifies that the House of Commons is sitting during the night, whilst during the day the Union Jack is flown from the Victoria Tower.

This has been the seat of government since the early part of the eleventh century but not until 1547 did it become the permanent home of Parliament. The present neo-Gothic buildings, dating from about 1850, are the work of Sir Charles Barry and Augustus Pugin replacing the earlier structure which was almost totally destroyed by fire in a single night on 16 October 1834. The medieval crypt and cloisters of St. Stephen's Chapel escaped the fire and were skilfully incorporated into the new building along with Westminster Hall which for six hundred years was the chief court of English Law. This great hall, with its fine timber roof spanning some 70 feet, was originally built by William Rufus in 1097 and restored by King Richard II in 1398. It has been the scene of much stirring history — from Coronation banquets to trials for high treason. It was here that Sir Thomas More, King Charles I, William Wallace, Guy Fawkes, the Earl of Essex and many others of high rank were sentenced to death.

The never-to-be-forgotten Gunpowder Plot of 1605 failed to blow up the Houses of Parliament but enemy bombing

in 1941 inflicted serious damage to the Commons. Much of the timber used in the reconstruction of the new chamber, opened in 1950, was given by Commonwealth countries.

The House of Lords, which providentially escaped the 1941 bombing is a sumptuous chamber in rich tones of red and gold and is the meeting place of the Lords Spiritual and the Lords Temporal. The walls are lined with paintings and with statues of the eighteen barons who secured the Magna Carta from King John in 1215. At the south end of the chamber is the magnificent Queen's Throne with its beautiful carved and gilt canopy — the smaller throne on the right is for the Consort. The Lord Chancellor, who presides over the assembly, sits on the Woolsack which signifies the former importance of wool to the economy of England.

The genius of Pugin's ornamentation in the grand Gothic style is richly portrayed in the Queen's Robing Room, a sumptuous state apartment replete with elaborate woodcarving and containing a series of paintings by William Dyce depicting the legend of King Arthur. The adjacent Royal Gallery, a long room with a fine coloured Minton tiled floor, is dominated by two huge paintings; *The Death of Nelson* and *The Meeting of Wellington and Blucher after Waterloo* by Daniel Maclise and contains gilt statues of every monarch from King Alfred to Queen Anne.

The Palace of Westminster.

The Royal Gallery.

The House of Commons (bottom).

"Cutty Sark" (top).

Canaletto's View of Greenwich from the Isle of Dogs (bottom).

GREENWICH

Some five miles down river from Tower Bridge, on the south bank, Greenwich has a unique place in English maritime history. It was a modest fishing hamlet in the Middle Ages, when Humphrey, Duke of Gloucester, decided to build a house here in which he kept his celebrated library, later to be the foundation for Oxford's Bodleian. Subsequent Kings and Queens established Greenwich as their favourite royal palace outside London. Henry VII patronised Greenwich and fought the Cornish rebels on nearby Blackheath in 1497. Henry VIII was born here, as were his daughters Mary Tudor and Elizabeth I. He married Anne Boleyn at Greenwich in 1533 but only three years later, during a tournament in Greenwich Park, signed her death warrant for suspected infidelity. Henry VIII also married Anne of Cleves at Greenwich Palace in 1540. The young Edward VI spent much of his short life here and Elizabeth I shared her father's love of Greenwich. It was from Greenwich Palace that Queen Elizabeth I, in June 1588, despatched her messengers with orders for the defence of the realm against the long-awaited and then imminent Spanish invasion which culminated in the naval victory off Calais.

Sir Walter Raleigh's immortal act of gallantry, when he spread his cloak over the mud for the Queen to walk on, was reputedly enacted on the site of the Queen's House. King James I commissioned Inigo Jones to build the Queen's House for Anne of Denmark in 1616. But it was Henrietta Maria, wife of Charles I who occupied it first in 1637, and their son Charles II allowed her to return there after the Restoration.

Flamsteed House (the Old Royal Observatory).

The Queen's House, is the first and finest example of Palladian architecture in England. Its fundamental simplicity of line is as refreshing today as it was undoubtedly revolutionary to Jones's contemporaries who were more accustomed to Jacobean fussiness. The Great Hall, which opens onto all parts of the House, is a giant cube with a richly carved and beamed ceiling. The remarkable black and white marble floor by Nicholas Stone, is best viewed from the gallery, reached by an exquisite wrought-iron circular staircase adorned with tulip-like scroll work. The House today contains a rich collection of paintings by Kneller, Van Dyck, Van de Velde, Canaletto and Lely, fine period furniture, and elaborately plastered ceilings.

The colonnade were added between 1807-16 to commemorate Nelson's victory at Trafalgar, and linked the buildings which were opened in 1937 as the National Maritime Museum, housing a unique collection of British maritime history from Tudor times to the present day. The great discoveries of naval science and exploration are illustrated through prints, books, models, figureheads, relics, instruments of navigation, boats and paintings by such masters as Hogarth, Gainsborough, Reynolds, Turner and Romney.

On the other side of the road, fronting the River, stands the impressive group of buildings which is now the Royal Naval College. It was originally intended by Charles II as an extension of the new palace to vie with Louis XIV's Palace of Versailles, but only the north-west wing was completed, and in 1692 William and Mary decided that the needs of disabled and retired seamen were more pressing and ordered the building to be completed as a hospital under the guidance of Sir Christopher Wren. The hospital was opened in 1705, but it took another forty-five years to complete, during which time Hawksmoor, Vanburgh and finally Ripley took over Wren's mantle and each contributed to making the complex of hospital buildings described by Sir Charles Reilly as "the most stately procession of buildings we possess". These are best viewed from the Isle of Dogs on the other side of the river, as depicted in Canaletto's famous painting.

The Painted Hall, designed by Wren, has a painted ceiling surpassed in Europe only by that of the Sistine Chapel. This superb masterpiece is the work of Sir James Thornhill which he started in 1708 and took nearly twenty years to complete. The painting contains over two hundred figures surrounding portraits of William and Mary. It was to this hall that Nelson's body was brought after the Battle of Trafalgar in 1805.

The beautiful Chapel nearby dates from 1752 but the original built to Wren's design was largely destroyed by fire in 1799. It was subsequently restored by James Stuart.

The Royal Observatory, standing high on the hill overlooking these splendid buildings, was built by Wren at the command of Charles II in 1675 to assist navigation, and is known throughout the world for the first accurate determination of Mean Time. The zero meridian of longitude is marked by a brass strip in the courtyard and it is thus possible to stand with a foot in both the western and eastern hemispheres. Its contribution to accurate time-keeping and navigation was invaluable.

Much of the work dealing with astronomical observation was transferred to Hurstmonceux Castle, Sussex, in 1948, and Flamsteed House (named after the first Astronomer Royal) is today part of the National Maritime Museum concerned with navigation and astronomy.

Every day at 13.00 hours precisely a red ball mounted on a mast on the east turret falls as a visual time signal for ships on the Thames, as it has done regularly since 1833. *The Cutty Sark,* one of the world's most famous sailing ships, is the last survivor of the tea-clippers, built in 1869 and dry-docked near Greenwich pier in 1957. This incredible vessel carried 32,000 square feet of sail and could cover over 350 miles a day. On board is a nautical museum and a fascinating collection of ships' figureheads.

Close by is *Gypsy Moth IV* in which Sir Francis Chichester sailed around the world single-handed in 1966-67.

The ceremony of Trooping the Colour on Horse Guard's Parade: the splendour of the Sovereign's Birthday Parade.

The Life Guards of the Household Cavalry.

Mounted sentries at Horse Guards are provided by troopers of The Life Guards (left) and (right) the Blues and Royals.

POMP, PAGEANTRY AND CEREMONIES

No ceremony is more popular than the ancient and mysterious ceremony of *Trooping the Colour*. This splendid and colourful event in honour of the Sovereign's official birthday is held annually on the first or second Saturday in June.

The route from Buckingham Palace to Horse Guards Parade, behind Whitehall, is decorated with banners and flags and lined with thousands of spectators, eagerly waiting to see the Queen heading the procession, dressed in uniform and riding side-saddle on one of her favourite horses.

The troops, in full dress uniforms, are from the Household Cavalry and the Guards Division. Two separate mounted regiments make up the Corps of Household Cavalry; the Life Guards originating from the time of King Charles I, who wear scarlet tunics with white plumed helmets, and the Blues and Royals (formerly the Royal Horse Guards) with blue tunics and red plumed helmets, who were a regiment during the Cromwellian period. These regiments share the honour of providing a personal bodyguard for the Sovereign on all state occasions.

Five separate regiments comprise the Guards Division, all of whom wear scarlet tunics and bearskins: the Grenadiers (1656) are distinguished by a scarlet hatband with a white plumed bearskin; the Coldstream (1650) have a scarlet plume in their bearskins and a white hatband; the Scots Guards (1642) hatbands are chequered red, white and blue but no plumes; the Irish Guards (1900) wear a pale blue feather plume in their bearskin

The Royal family on the balcony of Buckingham Palace acknowledge the cheering crowds below.

The Scots Guards arriving to change the guard at Buckingham Palace.

and a green hatband; whilst the fifth and youngest regiment, the Welsh Guards (1915) have a black hatband with a white, green and white feather in their bearskin plume. The Guards also perform guard duties at Buckingham Palace, St. James's Palace and Clarence House. The sheer mass of dazzling colour, the music of the mounted bands, the precision marching and counter-marching, are truly an experience never to be forgotten.

Changing the Guard is another colourful ceremony which takes place most mornings in the courtyard of the Horse Guards, Whitehall, by the Queen's Life Guard from the Household Cavalry. At Buckingham Palace the guard is changed by the Queen's Guard, provided by the Guards division.

Royal Salutes are fired on special occasions such as the Queen's official birthday (marked also by Trooping the Colour), royal births, State Openings of Parliament, and to honour visiting royalty and heads of state. The King's Troop, Royal Horse Artillery, has the privilege of firing salutes in Hyde Park when 41 guns are fired. At the Tower of London the Honourable Artillery Company, the oldest British regiment, fires 62 guns.

The State Opening of Parliament is an annual event, usually towards the end of October or early November or following a general election. The Queen drives from Buckingham Palace in the Irish State Coach, accompanied by a sovereign's mounted escort, by way of The Mall to the House of Lords. The Queen's Speech from the throne in the House of Lords (the sovereign has not been admitted to the Commons for over three hundred years since King Charles I was refused entry), traditionally sets the theme of the Government's business for the ensuing session.

The Lord Mayor's Show is a delightful pageant of great historic interest dating as it does from at least 1378. Its original purpose was to show the new Lord Mayor to the citizens of the City and to receive approval from the monarch. In former days the newly-elected Lord Mayor had to travel for this purpose to the Palace of Westminster but today the ritual takes place at the Temple Bar, the City boundary on the western side, outside the Law Courts, where he is greeted by the Lord Chief Justice as representative of the monarch.

The Lord Mayor rides in an elaborately gilded coach, built in 1756, and weighing nearly four tons, needing six strong horses to draw it. The procession leaves from the Guildhall, goes along Cheapside, to the Law Courts and returns by way of the Embankment to the Mansion House where a banquet is held in his honour. It has always been held a month following the October election and in recent years on the second Saturday of November, so as to avoid adding to London's traffic problems. Traditionally the groups forming the procession are chosen by the Lord Mayor to feature a theme of topical interest.

The Lord Mayor's coach and Pikemen of the Honourable Artillery Company.

H.M.S. "Discovery".

LONDON'S RIVER

London was conceived along the banks of the Thames and over the centuries this, the most famous of all rivers, became the main artery serving the heart of the greatest city in the Western hemisphere. For over five hundred years the Thames was London's main highway connecting Westminster to The Tower and the royal palaces at Greenwich and Hampton Court. Although no longer the world's busiest port nor even the largest city, London retains its unique character and is still the commercial and financial centre of the world.

The river-scene has changed greatly since Canaletto painted his memorable views of its incomparable sky-line of church spires but London is still best viewed from its river, and a regular service of pleasure trips is operated during the summer months down to Greenwich from Charing Cross Pier and upstream from Westminster to Richmond and Hampton Court.

Downstream the last bridge to cross the river is Tower Bridge, that famous landmark and triumph of Victorian engineering, opened in 1894. The two enormous bascules, connecting the north and south banks, weigh about 1,000 tons each and are raised to allow the larger ships to pass upstream into the famous Pool of London.

This feat takes only one-and-a-half minutes and to the credit of the designers, Sir Horace Jones and Sir John Wolfe Barry, the machinery has rarely failed.

H.M.S. *Belfast,* permanently moored on the south bank, opposite the Tower of London, is the largest and most powerful cruiser ever built for the Royal Navy. Now open to the public it houses a Royal Navy Museum. Next comes the oldest of the Thames' crossings, London Bridge, of nursery rhyme fame, "London Bridge is falling down..." It is thought the Romans built a crossing here but the first stone bridge dates from about 1209 and this had nineteen arches with houses, shops, a chapel in the middle, and fortified gates on each bank on the spikes of which were fixed the heads of executed traitors. The narrow arches restricted the tidal flow and in hard winters the Thames used to freeze over which allowed Frost Fairs to be held on the ice. In the severe winter of 1683-84 an ox was roasted on the ice as part of the celebrations. A new bridge was built in 1832 and this lasted until 1968 when it proved inadequate for the demands of twentieth-century traffic. The present concrete bridge was opened in 1973; its granite predecessor was sold to the Americans (who mistakenly thought they were getting Tower Bridge!) and re-erected in Arizona.

A masterpiece of British architecture, was the general

opinion of Denys Lasdun's design for the new National Theatre on the South Bank. After more than 100 years the dream has become reality at an estimated cost in excess of £ 15,000,000.

Waterloo Bridge was designed by Sir Giles Gilbert Scott and the engineers of the London County Council and only completed in 1945. This slim, graceful construction, of steel and concrete, is a worthy successor to John Rennie's famous stone bridge which was demolished in the 1930's.

The Royal Festival Hall is the focal point of the South Bank Arts Centre. Built in 1951 for the Festival of Britain it is deservedly acclaimed for its decor and outstanding acoustics. The Hayward Gallery, the Queen Elizabeth Hall, the Purcell Room and the National Film Theatre are the more recent additions.

Behind the Royal Festival Hall is the dominant Shell Centre, the largest office block in England, from which there are wonderful panoramic views of London to be had from the public gallery on the twenty-fifth floor.

Across the river is the Victoria Embankment, a most delightful riverside walk of one and a half miles, between Blackfriars and Westminster Bridges. The gardens are a feast of colour from spring right through summer. During the lunch hour visitors mingle with the office workers relaxing in deck chairs to the sweet strains of music from the band. The Watergate, near Embankment Underground Station (formerly Charing Cross) and Villiers Street, was originally the riverside entrance to York House gardens where lived the ill-fated Duke of Buckingham, friend of King Charles I, and shows the former extent of the river before the Embankment was built on reclaimed land in the second half of the nineteenth century. All that can be said with any certainty is that the Gate was built about 1626 by Nicholas Stone to a design by either Inigo Jones or Balthasar Gerbier. Behind the gardens is the unmistakable square-shaped Shell-Mex House (1931) with a massive clock rivalling Westminster's Big Ben in size. The neighbouring Savoy Hotel was built by Richard D'Oyly Carte in 1899 on the site of the Hospital (1505) and the Palace (*circa* 1246) of the Savoy.

There are four ships permanently moored to the Embankment: H.M.S. *President* and H.M.S. *Chrysanthemum* which serve as naval training ships of the London Royal Naval Reserve. H.M.S. *Wellington* a Second World War frigate, is unique in being the only floating livery hall, belonging to the Honourable Company of Master Mariners. H.M.S. *Discovery* was Captain Scott's polar research ship, launched in 1901 and first taken by him to Antartica in the same year. The manner in which Scott and his com-

The Royal Festival Hall.

panions perished, on the ill-fated Antarctic expedition in 1912, is a well-known story of gallantry.

Cleopatra's Needle, an obelisk of pink granite, sixty-eight feet high and weighing in excess of 190 tons, is peculiarly named being neither a needle nor having more than a passing connection with Queen Cleopatra. One of a pair dating from *circa* 1500 B.C. it came originally from the Temple of the Sun God at Heliopolis and was a gift from Mehemet Ali, Viceroy of Egypt, in 1819. Begrudgingly accepted, it was towed in 1867 to England and erected in 1878, after a perilous sea journey during which six seamen lost their lives. Its companion was given to New York and now stands in Central Park. The huge pair of bronze sphinxes at the base of the Needle were specifically designed for the site by G.F. Vulliamy.

Continuing up river, on the south bank, is County Hall, built for the London County Council between 1912 and 1932 and now the administrative headquarters of the Greater London Council. Outside County Hall stands the South Bank Lion, originally the trademark of the Lion Brewery. The lion is of particular interest because it was made in 1837 of Coade stone the secret formula of which, the most durable artificial stone ever invented, is lost forever.

The graceful cast-iron Westminster Bridge was constructed between 1854-62 to replace the earlier one of stone, the view from which inspired Wordsworth's famous sonnet:

Earth has not anything to show more fair:
Dull would he be of soul who could pass by,
A sight so touching in its majesty.

Queen Boadicea.

Westminster Bridge.

Lambeth Palace and the parish church of St. Mary.

The design blends well with the neo-Gothic of the Houses of Parliament. At the south end of the bridge is the bronze statue of Queen Boadicea by Thomas Thornycroft, unveiled in 1902. Boadicea, widow of the King of Iceni, rebelled against the Roman occupation and in A.D. 61 attacked the City which was razed to the ground and most of its inhabitants were slain. The professionally trained and better armed Roman army subsequently proved superior to the Britons who were slaughtered without mercy. Boadicea and her daughters took poison to avoid a more terrible death.

Across the river from the Houses of Parliament are the new buildings of St. Thomas's Hospital, founded in 1213 and moved to this site in 1868. Beyond the hospital, by Lambeth Bridge, is the irregular shape of Lambeth Palace, the official London residence of the Archbishops of Canterbury for over 750 years. The red brick gatehouse was built by Bishop Morton in about 1495 and is a superb example of early Tudor brickwork. The Great Hall, largely destroyed during the time of Cromwell, was rebuilt by Archbishop Juxon in 1663. The hall has a magnificent hammer-beam roof and contains an important library with some finely illuminated manuscripts. The Lollards' Tower, *circa* 1450, supposedly commemorates the followers of John Wycliffe (1320-1384). The undercroft, or vaulted crypt, below the Chapel is the oldest part of the Palace dating from the early thirteenth century, whilst the Chapel itself has been extensively restored as the result of severe damage during the last war. The Guard Room has a fourteenth-century timber roof and contains a rich collection of paintings, including portraits by Holbein and Van Dyck. Nearby the south gateway is the parish church of St. Mary, which was rebuilt in 1851. Only the Kentish ragstone west tower remains from the earlier fourteenth-century building. Buried here are Elias Ashmole, the antiquarian, Archbishops Bancroft and Tenison and the infamous Captain Bligh of the *Bounty.*

Beyond Lambeth Bridge, on the north bank, is the

towering Vickers Building (1963), a superb curved-shaped office block of reinforced concrete and stainless steel, rising to 387 feet. Between this elegant skyscraper and Vauxhall Bridge (1816, one of the first to be built of iron) is the Tate Gallery.

The next bridge upstream is the graceful Chelsea Bridge (1937), and just past it, set back on the north bank, is Chelsea Royal Hospital. According to legend, Nell Gwynn persuaded King Charles II to build it, but it is likely that the idea was suggested to him by Louis XIV's Hôtel des Invalides, built some ten years previously in Paris. The Chelsea Royal Hospital was designed by Sir Christopher Wren who worked on it from 1682 to 1691, with later additions by Robert Adam between 1765 and 1792 and finally completed by Sir John Soane. The Chapel and Central Court are very much as Wren left them and represent some of his best extant secular work. In the courtyard is the bronze statue of Charles II in Roman dress which is said to be by Grinling Gibbons. Every year on Oak Apple Day (May 19th, Charles II birthday) the statue is decora-

ted with oak leaves to commemorate the tree in which he hid during his escape after the battle of Worcester. The two main wings projecting towards the river house some 500 old and disabled soldiers, the beloved Chelsea Pensioners, resplendent in their eighteenth-century soldiers' uniform with scarlet coats in the summer and dark blue in the winter. The hospital grounds are the setting for the Chelsea Flower Show, held annualy towards the end of May.

Facing the hospital on the opposite bank is the beautiful Battersea Park, which offers a Funfair, boating lake and a children's zoo. The gardens and river frontage, the latter leading along to the Albert Bridge (1873) interesting for its unusual combination of suspension and cantilever principles of construction, are floodlit during the summer evenings.

The heavy iron Battersea Bridge (1890) replaced the earlier wooden one immortalised in Whistler's painting, *Nocturne in Black and Gold,* which was the subject of a famous libel action brought by the artist against John

Lambeth Bridge.

Albert Bridge.

Ruskin. Whistler won but was awarded only one farthing by way of damages, and had to bear crippling legal costs. Putney Bridge is the starting point of the annual Boat Race between rowing eights from Oxford and Cambridge Universities. The race is held on a Saturday about Easter-time, over a $4\frac{1}{4}$ mile course between Putney Bridge and Mortlake. First rowed at Henley in 1829 and here since 1856, the Boat Race still attracts world-wide interest. Immediately before Kew Bridge, on the north bank, is the charming riverside village of Strand-on-the-Green, whilst just beyond the bridge on the south side of the river are the Royal Botanic Gardens, better known to Londoners as Kew Gardens. This is a delightful place to visit, particularly in spring and early summer to see the acres of magnifi-

cent flowering shrubs and spring flowers. In fact the gardens, dating back to 1759, are a scientific establishment occupying nearly 300 acres in which some 45,000 trees, herbs, shrubs and flowers are grown along with numerous tropical species in giant glasshouses. The curious-looking Pagoda was built in 1762 and reflects the then current oriental interst. Near the Temperate House is the tallest flagpole in the world, 225 feet high. Kew Palace, or the Dutch House, shows another period fashion in architecture. It was built in 1631 and was much favoured by King George III and Queen Charlotte.
Beyond the elegant bridge at Richmond is Hampton Court, which Cardinal Wolsey, no doubt in an effort to halt his fall from favour, presented to King Henry VIII but, as

Hampton Court Palace: the Great Gatehouse.

Clock Court (right), the Maze (far right) and (bottom right) Fountain Court.

Hampton Court: the Queen's Drawing Room.

history records, to no avail. Built between 1515 and 1520 as Wolsey's private residence, this was to become the most beautiful royal palace in the land. Successive royal occupants enlarged it; first Henry VIII who added the Great Hall, Chapel and laid the first tennis court in England. Henry VIII brought five of his wives in turn to live here as Queen and according to legend the ghosts of two of them, Jane Seymour and Catherine Howard, still haunt the Palace. King Edward VI, Mary Tudor, Queen Elizabeth I, King James I, King Charles I (it was both his home and his prison) and King Charles II held court here. The next major reconstruction was carried out by Sir Christopher Wren during the reign of King William and Queen Mary. The Wren additions include the Fountain Court and garden front. Through the second courtyard and over the Anne Boleyn Gateway is the curious astronomical clock erected in 1540 and still in working order. The Great Vine

is reputed to have been planted in 1769 and the famous Maze, 6 feet high and 2 feet thick, probably dates from the reign of King William and Queen Mary.

Most of the buildings are open to the public, and have been since 1839 by order of Queen Victoria, the only exceptions being the "grace and favour" residences granted to distinguished servants of the Crown and their dependants.

The Palace's art collection includes such masterpieces as Titian's *Jacopo Sannazaro* (Portrait of a Man), *Apollo and the Nine Muses* by Tintoretto, Correggio's *Virgin and Child,* a rare religious painting by Holbein, *Noli me Tangere* and Bellini's *Portrait of a Man* as well as major works by Van Dyck, Lely and Kneller.

Few places in England can match Hampton Court's historical associations, its architecture and art treasures, or the beautiful landscaped gardens.

The tomb of Rahere: St. Bartholomew the Great.

LONDON'S CHURCHES AND PLACES OF RELIGIOUS INTEREST

Pride of place must undoubtedly go to Westminster Abbey and St. Paul's Cathedral, but London has a wealth of fine churches, including some of Saxon or Norman origins. Tragically, so many were destroyed during the Great Fire (1666) and of those that survived or were rebuilt by Sir Christopher Wren, designer of over fifty London churches, many suffered again during the Second World War, necessitating another massive programme of restoration and rebuilding. Among those of particular interest are:

St. Bartholomew the Great, Smithfield. This is the City's oldest surviving church, being the remains of the Priory of St. Bartholomew founded about 1123 by Rahere who also established London's first hospital nearby. The brick tower, containing the oldest complete ring of bells in London, was built during the seventeenth century. Among a wealth of historic monuments in this church the most outstanding is the tomb and effigy of Rahere. The font in the Lady Chapel is reputed to be the only medieval one remaining in the City and was used for Hogarth's baptism in 1697.

All Hallows, Barking-by-the-Tower. Of Saxon origin, this church survived the Great Fire but suffered much damage in the Second World War. Famous now as the Church of Toc H, which was founded by the Rev. P.B. ("Tubby") Clayton in Flanders during the First World War, the present church was rebuilt by subscriptions from all over the world and re-dedicated in 1957. In the crypt are the remains of a Roman tessellated pavement, parts of the original Saxon walls and a museum. From the top of its brick tower, built in 1659, Samuel Pepys surveyed the Great Fire. William Penn was baptised here in 1644.

St. Bride's. This is the parish church of Fleet Street printers and journalists. It is a fine example of Wren architecture, which like so many others suffered almost total destruction in 1940. Only the beautiful tower and multi-tiered spire ("a madrigal in stone") survived. Post-war excavations revealing evidence of no less than seven earlier churches on this site are displayed in the crypt. In 1957 this church was carefully restored to Wren's original plans.

St. Dunstan-in-the-West, Fleet Street. This was rebuilt to an unusual octagonal plan in the Gothic Style by John Shaw in 1831. In the earlier church, which survived the Great Fire, William Tyndale preached, as did the poet John Donne. Izaak Walton (author of *The Compleat Angler,* 1653) was a vestryman here. Outside the church, to the right of its tower, which dominates Fleet Street, is a fascinating clock made in 1671 with two giant figures which strike the hours and quarters; there is also a contemporary statue of Queen Elizabeth I which originally adorned Lud Gate.

St. Etheldreda, Ely Place, Holborn. The only pre-Reformation church in London which has been restored to Roman Catholicism. Dating from about 1290 it was originally a private chapel for the Bishops of Ely.

Wesley's House and Chapel, City Road. The home of John Wesley, founder of Methodism, for the last years of his life. The house is now a museum containing personal relics of John and his brother, Charles, and is visited by Methodists from all over the world. The chapel, founded in 1778, was rebuilt in 1899.

St. Bride's.

St. Dunstan-in-the-West.

Queen Elizabeth I.

Brompton Oratory, Knightsbridge (The Church of the London Oratory of St. Philip Neri). This was designed by Herbert Gribble in 1878 and built in the Italian Baroque style. The magnificent interior contains gigantic marble statues of the Apostles, dating from the seventeenth century and which originally stood in Siena Cathedral. The Church is noted for its choral recitals and fine music.

St. Clement Danes, Strand. The church was rebuilt by Wren in 1680-82 on the site of a medieval church, though the spire was not added until 1719. Only the walls and tower survived the bombing of London in 1941. Restored in the mid 1950's as the official church of the Royal Air Force. Well known for its bells ("Oranges and lemons, say the bells of St. Clement's") and the association with Dr. Johnson, whose statue stands outside at the east end facing Fleet Street.

St. Stephen Walbroook. This City church is held to be among Wren's finest works with a dome designed on a similar theme to that of St. Paul's. Built between 1672 and 1679 in Baroque style, St. Stephen's is the Lord Mayor's parish church. The rather drab exterior belies the elegance of the interior with its Corinthian pillars and period fittings, including the richly carved reredos, the stone font, with a wooden cover and a pulpit with a decorated canopy.

The Spanish and Portuguese Synagogue, Bevis Marks, City. Unique for its fine state of preservation and being the first synagogue to be built after the Jews were allowed to resettle by Oliver Cromwell in 1657, following an enforced absence of 365 years. Built by Joseph Avis, a Quaker, in 1701.

Brompton Oratory.

St. Clement Danes.

Doctor Johnson.

St. Mary-le-Bow, Cheapside. The famous Bow Bells, which caused Dick Whittington to turn again, and within the sound of which Londoners must be born to qualify as true Cockneys, were destroyed by enemy action in 1941 along with much of the church which was built by Wren between 1670 and 1683. The interior has been re-built to Wren's design, and a new peal of bells cast which were first rung by Prince Philip in 1961. The steeple is particularly noteworthy with its unusually high and square

St. Margaret's, Westminster and (below) *Southwark Cathedral.*

tower. The name "le Bow" comes from the bows or arches of the earlier Norman crypt. A piazza occupies the site of the old churchyard with a modern statue of Captain John Smith, Governor of Virginia who was rescued by Pocahontas, the little Indian princess.

St. Martin-in-the-Fields, Trafalgar Square. Built in 1726 by Wren's pupil James Gibb. Apart from the beautiful ceiling of Italian workmanship, the remainder of the interior is severely classical. The magnificent portico, bearing the Royal Arms, is supported by six giant Corinthian columns and approached by a wide flight of steps.

St. Margaret's, nearby Westminster Abbey. St. Margaret's has been the parish church of the House of Commons since 1614. According to tradition the original church was founded by Edward the Confessor in the twelfth century but the present building dates from 1523. The fine Flemish glass of the east window was a betrothal present from Ferdinand and Isabella of Spain to Prince Arthur, son of Henry VII, and their daughter, Katharine of Aragon. Unfortunately poor Arthur died and his brother, later to become Henry VIII, had married his widowed sister-in-law before the gift arrived. It was not until 1758 that the glass was installed in St. Margaret's. Among the famous persons buried here are Sir Walter Raleigh, William Caxton, and Admiral Hollar Blake. Those married here include Samuel Pepys (1655), John Milton (1656) and Winston Churchill (1908).

Southwark Cathedral, Borough High Street. Despite its twelfth century origins it has only been a Cathedral since 1905. One of the finest specimens of Gothic buildings in London, with Norman remains and a splendid Early English Lady Chapel. The reredos was a gift in 1520 from Bishop Fox of Winchester who also founded Corpus Christi at Oxford. The Harvard Memorial Chapel, formerly the Chapel of St. John the Evangelist, was restored by Harvard University in 1907 in honour of its founder, John Harvard, who was baptized here in 1608. Among the many fine and interesting monuments is a modern one to Shakespeare (his younger brother, Edmund, was buried here in 1607); poet John Gower (1408); Lancelot Andrewes, Bishop of Winchester, who died in 1626; Lionel Lockyer (1672), etc.

Westminster Cathedral, off Victoria Street. The Cathedral is the principal Roman Catholic church in England and the seat of the Cardinal Archbishop of Westminster. Designed by John Francis Bentley in Byzantine style, it was begun in 1895 and completed in 1903. The campanile is 284 feet high and from its gallery, reached by a lift, the visitor has a magnificent view of London. The interior is largely unfinished but eventually will be lined with marble and mosaic, as are some of the side chapels. Of particular interest are the distinguished bas-reliefs of Eric Gill depicting the Stations of the Cross. Recent rebuilding in Victoria Street provides, for the first time, a fine uninterrupted view of the exterior.

Westminster
Cathedral.

Looking east along the nave.

Chapel of St Gregory and St. Augustine.

One of fourteen Stations of the Cross by Eric Gill

British Museum: the Reading Room.

THE ARTS: MUSEUMS, GALLERIES AND COLLECTIONS

London is a repository of the world's artistic and historical treasures. In its many art galleries and museums, housed in elegant surroundings, one can see a fully comprehensive range of paintings, sculptures, archaeological discoveries, historical documents, manuscripts and the printed word — the arts and artefacts of mankind from his beginnings to the present day.

The British Museum, Bloomsbury, is the world's largest and most important museum. Built between 1823 and 1847 by brothers Sydney and Robert Smirke, its origins owe much to the generosity of Sir Robert Cotton and Sir Hans Sloane. The museum has three major divisions: The National Library, Prints and Drawings, and Archaeology. The magnificent domed Reading Room is used by students from all over the world and it. was here that Karl Marx researched for *Das Kapital.*

The museum has an unsurpassed collection of illuminated manuscripts, original documents, letters, and many examples of fine bindings. Typical of its collection: The Lindisfarne Gospels, Nelson's last letter to Emma Hamilton, the Gutenberg Bible of 1454, Shakespeare's First Folio of 1623, and an original copy of the Magna Carta. Among the important archaeological exhibits are the Portland Vase, smashed by a Victorian madman but subsequently skilfully restored, the Sutton Hoo Treasure, Egyptian mummies, the Rosetta Stone, and the Elgin Marbles.

The Ethnographical Department, renamed the Museum of Mankind, devoted to the art and culture of primitive peoples is temporarily housed at Burlington Gardens, behind the Royal Academy in Piccadilly.

The Tate Gallery, Millbank, is the national gallery of British Art with a wide-ranging collection of the modern continental schools of painting and sculpture. Its incomparable art collection includes sculptures by Rodin, Eric Gill, Modigliani, Degas, Picasso, Epstein, Henry Moore, Barbara Hepworth and Reg Butler. Paintings by Lely *(Elizabeth, Countess of Kildare)*, Reynolds *(The Age of Innocence)*, Stubbs *(A Hound and a Bitch)*, Blake (a large collection of his drawings, paintings and watercolours), Turner (no less than five galleries are devoted to this artist), Constable *(Dedham Mill)*, Gainsborough *(Giovanna Baccelli)*, a good showing of the Pre-Raphaelite school in works by Hunt *(Strayed Sheep)*, Millais *(Ophelia)* and Rossetti *(The Girlhood of Mary Virgin)*, and Ford Maddox Brown *(The Last of England)*; Whistler *(Nocturne in Black and Gold)*, Manet *(Woman With a Cat)*, Monet *(Poplars on the Epte)*, Cezanne *(The Gardener)*, Gauguin *(Harvest)*, Van Gogh *(The Chair and the Pipe)*, Matisse *(Nude Study in Blue)*, Picasso *(Woman in a Chemise)*, Lowry *(Old House, Salford)* and every conceivable — some would say inconceivable as well — form of modernisms.

The Tate regularly holds special exhibitions featuring the work of a single artist or school of painting.

The Tate Gallery.

A Hound and a Bitch *by George Stubbs.*

Royal Academy: Michelangelo's sculptured tondo.

Royal Academy of Arts, Piccadilly was founded in 1768 under the patronage of King George III and has been established at Burlington House for over a hundred years. Its permanent collection includes Michelangelo's sculptured tondo *The Virgin and Child and St John,* paintings by Constable, Turner, Millais, Sickert, Reynolds etc., but the Academy is principally known for the opportunity it gives to British artists of submitting work for display, without charge, at regular Summer and Winter exhibitions.

The Small
Meadow
in Spring
*by Alfred
Sisley.*

La Place
du Tertre
*by Maurice
Utrillo.*

Constable's
Haywain.

The National Gallery.

The National Gallery, Trafalgar Square, was opened to the public in 1824, it was then situated in Pall Mall, whilst the present building dates from 1838. From relatively humble beginnings, based on John Julius Angerstein's collection of 38 paintings purchased by the government of the day, the National now ranks as one of the world's most important art galleries in terms of range and quality. Its comprehensive collection, representing painters of all schools, ranges from the thirteenth to the early twentieth century and includes such treasures as Fra Angelico's *Christ Glorified in the Court of Heaven, Mystic Nativity* by Botticelli (the only known signed painting by this artist), in a room to itself Leonardo da Vinci's *Virgin and Child,* Giorgione's *Adoration of the Magi,* Titian's *Bacchus and Ariadne,* Canaletto's *The Stonemason's Yard,* van Eyck's *Arnolfini Marriage Portrait,* Rubens' *The Rape of the Sabine Women,* Vermeer's *Lady Standing at a Virginal,* Velazquez's *Immaculate Conception,* El Greco's *Agony in the Garden,* Monet's *Waterlilies,* Seurat's *Une Baignade, Asnières,* Gainsborough's *The Painter's Daughters* and Constable's *Haywain.* An uncatalogued attraction is the talented art of the pavement artists, or 'screevers', much in evidence outside both the National Gallery and National Portrait Gallery around the corner in St. Martin's Place.

Mrs. Siddons as the Tragic Muse *by Reynolds.*

Two Dancers on a Stage *by Degas.*

Courtauld Institute Galleries, Woburn Square, houses the many art treasures bequeathed to the University of London. Notable for its remarkable Courtauld collection of Impressionist and Post-Impressionist art: Daumier, Degas, Renoir, Manet, Monet, Pissarro, Cézanne, Van Gogh, Gauguin, Modigliani, Utrillo, Toulouse-Lautrec, Seurat, etc. Also the Lee collection of fourteenth and fifteenth century paintings, and the Gambier-Parry bequest of early Italian paintings, glass, enamels and ivories.

Dulwich College Picture Gallery (sometimes overlooked for not being in central London) in the heart of a south-eastern suburb, owes its origins to a bequest of actor Edward Alleyn (1566-1626) and was one of London's first public art galleries. Outstanding in its fine collection are Rembrandt's *A girl at a Window,* several sketches by Rubens, Van Dyck's *Lady Venetia Digby on her Deathbed,* Poussin's *The Nurture of Jupiter,* Claude's *Jacob with Laban and his Daughters,* two religious panels by Raphael, Canaletto's *Old Walton Bridge,* Murillo's *Two Peasant Boys,* Reynolds' *Mrs Siddons* and Hogarth's *A Fishing Party.*

Sir John Soane's Museum, Lincoln's Inn Fields. Soane bought the building in 1811, restyled it as a residence and also to house his unusual collection of paintings, antiquities and architectural drawings. The collection, its arrangement, and the house are very much as they were in Soane's lifetime. The house contains some fine period furniture, over 20,000 architectural drawings, Italian and Grecian statuary and among the interesting collection of paintings are Hogarth's two famous series, *The Rake's Progress* and *The Election.*

The Iveagh Bequest, Kenwood, Hampstead. Kenwood House and its beautiful setting are just as much an attraction as the high quality of the paintings and furniture on display. Bequeathed to the nation by the late Earl of Iveagh in 1927, this fine Georgian house was remodelled by Robert Adam for the first Earl of Mansfield between 1767-9. The magnificent library is the best remaining specimen of Adam's work.

The fine collection of paintings include Reynolds' *Kitty Fisher,* Gainsborough's *Pink Lady,* Vermeer's *The Guitar Lady,* a self-portrait by Rembrandt, de Jongh's *Old London Bridge,* Stubbs' *Whistlejacket* and Romney's *Lady Hamilton.*

Wellington Museum, Apsley House, Hyde Park Corner was for many years the home of the first Duke of Wellington. The art collection comprises in the main either the spoils of war or the Duke's own purchases. As one might expect there is a distinct military bias with several representations of Napoleon including a large nude statue by Canova carved from a single block of white marble. The honours of victory are everywhere: swords, flags, shields, silver, plate, porcelain, medals etc. The captured works of art include three major paintings by Velazquez, Van Dyck, Ribera and Murillo.

Hogarth's The Orgy.

Canova's marble statue of Napoleon.

The Science Museum. Despite its name this is in fact one of, if not the, most popular museums in the world, appealing to scientist and layman, adults and children. The displays, many of them animated, illustrate the history of technology and science and their applications from earliest times to the present day. Who could fail to be impressed by "Puffing Billy" the world's oldest railway engine (1813), Stephensons "Rocket" (1839), the enormous mass of the old Great Western Railway's "Caerphilly Castle" (1925), the early motor cars and aeroplanes?

The Geological Museum is concerned with earth history and economic geology. Of special interest is its famous collection of gemstones.

The Victoria and Albert Museum, in a building designed by Sir Aston Webb and constructed at the end of Queen Victoria's reign has a very wide-ranging collection demonstrating fine and applied arts from all over the world. Here are displays of textiles, woodwork, costumes, armour, jewellery, clocks, musical instruments, ceramics, engravings, and prints. Among its treasures are the Raphael cartoons (1516), a fine collection of English miniatures, Constable's sketches and paintings, and complete room displays of English and French furniture.

The Wallace Collection, Hertford House, W1. One of the finest private collections of works of art, it was bequeathed to the nation by Lady Wallace in 1897 and is displayed in a splendid late eighteenth-century town house.

The impressive collection ranges from paintings by Rembrandt, Titian, Canaletto, Van Dyck, Turner, Velazquez, Boucher, Hals, Watteau, Delacroix, Reynolds, etc., to sculpture, enamels, medals, armour, porcelain (Sèvres in particular) and French furniture.

Madame Tussaud's, Marylebone, NW1, is the world famous waxworks established here about 1833 when some of its first exhibits included deathmasks of guillotine victims from the French Revolution. Here the visitor may wander through the pages of history and mingle with the famous and infamous. An international display of Kings, Queens, politicians, stars of films, television and pop, sportsmen and women, all portrayed with an uncanny realism. There is great accuracy of detail and authentic clothing — often given from the wardrobe of the person depicted. Most of the figures — historic and modern — were modelled from life.

A recent innovation is the *son et lumière* Battle of Trafalgar tableaux with the added realism of the smell and smoke of gunpowder. The aptly named Chamber of Horrors is definitely not for the squeamish!

Next door, under a green copper dome, is *The Planetarium,* where the wonders of the heavens are displayed by means of an ingenious projector, accompanied by an interesting commentary.

There are no less than four museums in South Kensington: *The Natural History Museum* has one of the world's best collections of plants, animals, minerals, rocks, fossils and a splendid related library. The reconstructed skeleton of a dinosaur *Diplodocus* (84$\frac{1}{2}$ feet long) and the 90 foot blue whale always bring forth gasps of astonishment from the visitor who never before can have experienced anything of such frightening proportions.

◁ The Adam Library: Iveagh Bequest.

Natural History Museum: Diplodocus (right),
Geological Museum: collection of opals
(below), *(facing page)* Victoria & Albert
Museum: Tipu's Tiger (top), *and Science*
Museum: "Puffing Billy" (bottom).

Madame Tussauds and the Planetarium.

Queen Elizabeth I.

King Henry VIII and his six wives.

(Facing page): *Battle of Trafalgar* (top left) *Winston Churchill, J.F. Kennedy and Pope John XXIII* (bottom left) *the Guillotine* (top right), *and Pablo Picasso* (bottom right).

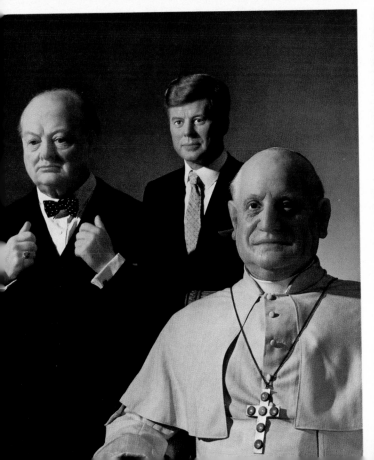

BUILDINGS: HISTORIC AND CONTEMPORARY

Despite the extensive development that has changed London's pre-war skyline almost beyond recognition, the best of its administrative, commercial, and domestic building is more historic than modern.

Buckingham Palace, the building known to all as the Queen's official London home, is a mixture of old and new. The original house built for the Duke of Buckingham in 1703 was substantially remodelled by John Nash in Palladian style 125 years later. The façade facing the Mall was added by Sir Aston Webb as recently as 1913. On her succession to the throne in 1837, Queen Victoria made Buckingham Palace her permanent home — the first monarch to do so — and instituted the custom by which the Royal Standard is flown from the flagstaff to show that the sovereign is in residence.

The Queen's Gallery (entrance in Buckingham Palace Road) is open to the public and presents an ever-changing display of art treasures from the royal collection. Behind the Palace is the Royal Mews where the horses and coa-

The Laughing Cavalier *by Frans Hals.*

ches used on state occasions are stabled. Here are kept the Irish State Coach used for state openings of Parliament, which was bought by Queen Victoria in 1852; the Golden State coach designed for King George III and used for coronations; the Glass State coach of King George V used for royal weddings; along with a fascinating collection of barouches, landaus, carriages and a unique display of harness and trappings.

The elaborate Victoria Memorial in front of Buckingham Palace, the Mall and Admiralty Arch were all part of the nation's tribute to Queen Victoria, constructed between 1910-12. The Memorial comprises a seated figure of the Queen looking towards the Mall surrounded by several symbolic groups surmounted by the gilt winged figure of Victory supported by Courage and Constancy. The Mall is the wide tree-lined driveway linking Buckingham Palace with Trafalgar Square and is the best vantage point for viewing royal processions. Spanning the entrance to the Mall from Trafalgar Square is Admiralty Arch through the centre of which only the sovereign may pass.

The handsome stuccoed *Carlton House Terrace* was designed by John Nash as residences for the aristocracy

St. James's Palace: the Tudor Gatehouse.

St. James's Palace: the Chapel Royal.

and built in the 1830's. Its two blocks of houses are divided by the Duke of York's Steps, leading up to the 124 foot high Duke of York's Column, erected in 1833 as a memorial to King George III's second son. Contemporary critics said the lightning conductor on top of the Duke's bronze statue was a spike for his unpaid bills. Commander-in-Chief of the British Army from 1798 until his death in 1827, his name is perpetuated in the nursery rhyme "The grand old Duke of York, he had ten thousand men, he marched them up to the top of the hill and marched them down again".

St. James's Palace was the sovereign's London residence until supplanted by Buckingham Palace, and its former importance is still acknowledged by the fact that foreign ambassadors are accredited to the "Court of St. James's". King Henry VIII demolished the Norman leper hospital originally occupying the site and built himself a royal palace,

of which there remains today only the fine brick gate-tower, Guard Room, the Presence Chamber and the Chapel Royal, which has a magnificent painted ceiling attributed to Holbein. There are two Chapels Royal attached to the Palace, the second is in nearby Marlborough Gate, known as the Queen's Chapel after Henrietta Maria, wife of King Charles I. Designed by Inigo Jones (*circa* 1627), this little-known architectural treasure is of classic proportions with an ornate roof, Carolean panelling and royal pews. Appropriate to the setting the choirboys are still dressed in Tudor costumes of scarlet and gold.

The Palace is now occupied by Court officials including the Lord Chamberlain, and by members of the royal family. The sentries in full-dress uniform are usually provided from the Guards Division, but occasionally this honour is shared with visiting Commonwealth regiments. *Lancaster House,* Stable Yard, beside St. James's Palace

Horse Guards, Whitehall *(top left),* and Cenotaph *(top right),*
Nº. 10 Downing Street *(bottom left)* and the less familiar
Cabinet Room *(bottom right).*

Lancaster House.

Albert Memorial.

is a wonderful example of early Victorian architecture: externally it is solidly plain but inside a riot of extravagance. When the grand old Duke of York died in debt, the Marquess of Stafford took possession and completed the house in 1840. In 1912 it was purchased by Lord Leverhulme who renamed it Lancaster House, and gave it to the nation. For a while it was the home of the London Museum. Open to the public when not being used for official functions it is well worth a visit to see the famous double staircase and the ceiling paintings of the long gallery.

Whitehall is the street linking Trafalgar Square to Parliament Square and is known for its concentration of Government offices and historic buildings: Ministry of Defence, Ministry of Agriculture, the Home Office, the Treasury, the old Admiralty Building, the Lord Privy Seal's office, Horse Guards, the Banqueting Hall, and at the far end the Cenotaph.

The Banqueting Hall, designed by Inigo Jones in 1619 for King James I, is all that remains of Whitehall Palace. One of the first of London's buildings in the classic Italian tradition it was possibly also the first to be built of Portland stone. Rubens received £3,000 and a knighthood from King Charles I for the nine allegorical paintings which adorn the ceiling. Possibly the King saw the paintings on that icy cold January morning when he left the House by

Royal Albert Hall.

The Old Curiosity Shop (bottom left) Dicken's House (top right), and Queen Anne's Gate.

way of a first floor window on the way to the scaffold. Oliver Cromwell made much use of the Hall for the reception of visiting ambassadors and King Charles II was officially welcomed here by the House of Commons on his Restoration. Opposite is the more colourful *Horse Guards*, built between 1750 and 1760 to the design of William Kent on the site of the guardhouse to the Whitehall Palace. Here are to be found those very popular subjects for the tourists' photographs: the imperturbable mounted guard of the Household Cavalry.

Horse Guards Parade, the former tilt-yard of the old Palace, is on the other side of the central archway and there the annual ceremony of Trooping the Colour takes place on the sovereign's official birthday.

Downing Street, off Whitehall is undoubtedly the most famous street in London, for No. 10 is the official home of the Prime Minister and has been since Sir Robert Walpole took up residence in 1735 at the suggestion of King George II. No. 11 is occupied by the Chancellor of the Exchequer whilst No. 12 is the office of the government Chief Whip.

Albert Hall, Kensington Gore, was the pride of Victorian London and named after Queen Victoria's consort, the Royal Albert Hall of Arts and Sciences. The elliptical

Panoramic view from the Post Office Tower

domed building, completed in 1871, has a capacity of approximately 8,000 and now serves a variety of purposes, the most popular–despite its somewhat imperfect acoustics–being the annual Promenade Concerts founded by Sir Henry Wood.

Queen Anne's Gate, Westminster. A street of early eighteenth-century houses of brown brickwork and bright clean paintwork. Now mainly used for commercial purposes the houses are remarkably well preserved. Elaborate doors, wooden porches, elegant canopies, black iron railings, torch extinguishers (No. 26) and the statue of Queen Anne outside No. 13 make this one of the prettiest streets in London.

Somerset House, Strand, was named after the Duke of Somerset, Lord Protector and uncle of King Edward VI. He started to build a palace here in 1547 but five years later and before its completion, he was executed at the Tower. The Crown promptly sequestrated the property and later it became the home of Queen Henrietta Maria and of Queen Catherine of Braganza. Towards the end of the eighteenth century it was rebuilt to the design of Chambers. The splendid south front, 800 feet long in Palladian style was his creation and prior to the construction of the Victoria Embankment it was lapped by the Thames. The east (now King's College) and west wings were added between 1824 and 1856, to Chamber's original scheme.

Somerset House is currently the headquarters of the Inland Revenue, national repository of wills, birth, marriage and death certificates.

Legal London: Discreetly separating the political City of Westminster from the commercial City of London are the four medieval Inns of Court (Inner Temple, Middle Temple, Gray's Inn and Lincoln's Inn) the custodians of English law. Each jealously independent of the other they control both the teaching and the practice of law in England and Wales. Their historic buildings have been skilfully restored after extensive damage in two wars.

Strolling through the many narrow passage-ways, splendid courtyards and tranquil gardens isolated from the noise of London's traffic is a pleasure not to be missed.

The Old Curiosity Shop, Portsmouth Street, WC2. Currently an antique-cum-gift shop whose name is possibly its only connection with Charles Dickens. Nevertheless it is one of the few surviving Tudor houses in London. Dickens however did live at 48 Doughty Street, WC1 where between 1837 and 1839 he wrote *The Pickwick Papers, Oliver Twist, Nicholas Nickleby* and *Barnaby Rudge.* Dickens House was opened in 1925 as a museum to this great English novelist and contains an interesting collection of Dickensiana.

The George Inn, Borough High Street, Southwark. This famous coaching inn dating from 1554 was rebuilt to the original plan after a fire in 1677. Formerly the double tier of wooden galleries surrounded three sides of a courtyard, but two wings were demolished in 1889 and today only the south wing survives. Nearby is the site of the Tabard Inn from which Chaucer's pilgrims started their journey to the shrine of Thomas à Becket at Canterbury.

The George Inn.

The Post Office Tower.

The Wellington Arch. ▷

The Post Office Tower, Howland Street, W1 formerly was London's highest building, nearly 600 feet above ground level. Its purpose is to allow telecommunications uninterrupted by other modern tall buildings. A revolving restaurant near the top provides a novel and unique panoramic view of the capital.

Hyde Park.

Peter Pan, Kensington Gardens.

Hyde Park regulars.

THE PARKS AND SQUARES

Looking at a map the emerald patches of London's parks stand out like islands in the very centre of its vast sea of streets and buildings. Islands where the visitor may stroll at leisure oblivious of the frantic activity beyond. Nowhere better for this than *Hyde Park,* a delightful expanse of grass and woodland covering some 360 acres. Here are facilities for boating and sailing on the Serpentine (the artificial lake created by Queen Caroline, wife of King George II), swimming at the Lido, the gentle relaxation of listening to the band, or admiring the riders in Rotten Row *(Route du Roi).* That great British tradition of free speech is regularly displayed at Speakers' Corner near Marble Arch every Sunday afternoon — a lively entertainment indeed.

Marble Arch (1828) at the north-east corner of the park was designed for Buckingham Palace and removed when the splendid wrought-iron gates proved too narrow for the State Coach; further into the park are to be found two statues by Epstein: *Pan* at the Knightsbridge entrance and in the bird sanctuary *Rima* a memorial to W.H. Hudson the naturalist. The enormous bronze figure, somewhat curiously named Achilles, near Hyde Park Corner is a tribute to Wellington and is close to Apsley House, his former home which is maintained as a museum in his honour.

The crowned signpost is a reminder of the park's royal origins.

Just relaxing.

Kensington Palace:
the Orangery.

Kensington Palace:
the Sunken Garden.

Rennies' bridge across the Serpentine informally divides Hyde Park from *Kensington Gardens,* once the grounds of Kensington Palace. Still retaining some suggestion of their former privacy they are today a popular haunt for children. Here very appropriately is Sir George Frampton's beloved statue of Peter Pan and the Round Pond where children of all ages demonstrate their prowess with model boats and sailing yachts. Halfway along Lancaster walk is G.F. Watts' striking equestrian statue representing Physical Energy erected in 1907. Dividing the gardens from Kensington Palace is the Broad Walk a wide tree-lined avenue running north-south. Kensington Palace, a somewhat plain red-brick building, became a royal palace when King William III acquired it soon after his accession and engaged Wren to transform it into a royal residence. Further alterations were made by William Kent for King George I in the 1720's. Here in 1819 Queen Victoria was born and was living there when she succeeded to the throne in 1837.

Parts of the Palace are occupied by "grace and favour" residents but the State Rooms are open to the public. The free-standing Orangery (1704), for many years attributed

Kensington Palace: the King's Gallery.

Easter Parade (top left). *Regent's Park in springtime* (top right). *A performance of* Much Ado About Nothing *at the open air theatre, in Regent's Park* (bottom).

The Zoological Gardens, Regent's Park.

Inhabitants of the Zoological Gardens.

to Wren (or Hawksmoor) but more recently considered to be the work of Vanbrugh, contains some excellent carvings by Grinling Gibbons as does the Presence Chamber in the Palace itself.

St. James's Park is by far the prettiest, and the oldest of the royal parks and is a joy to walk in at any season of the year. Well-stocked flower beds, the lawns, trees, shrubs, tame waterfowl, and an ample supply of deckchairs for the foot-sore visitor complete its attraction. The skyline vista of the government offices looking eastward beyond Horse Guard's Parade forms a perfect back-cloth to the park.

Green Park, added to St. James's Park by King Charles II, is the smallest royal park in central London. Consisting mainly of grassland and trees it is a peaceful haven from Piccadilly's traffic.

If one is looking for all that is to be desired in a park then *Regent's Park* succeeds admirably. John Nash, who also re-modelled St. James's Park, designed Regent's Park and it was named thus in honour of the Prince Regent (later to become King George IV) and first opened to the public in 1838. Many of the splendid terraces of houses overlooking the park, particularly those in the Outer Circle, are the work of John Nash and his protégé, Decimus Burton. Queen Mary's Gardens in the Inner Circle of the park have an unsurpassed collection of roses which fill the air with their fragrance during the summer months when one may also enjoy performances of Shakespeare's plays at the nearby open-air theatre.

Other attractions are the yachting and boating facilities, tennis courts, plenty of playing fields, a children's boating pond, a restaurant, and of course the famous London Zoo.

The Zoological Gardens at the north end of the park are a great favourite with children, especially Pet's Corner, and one may be forgiven for overlooking that its principal objective is scientific. Opened in 1828 the Zoo houses a collection of some 7,000 reptiles, birds, mammals, fishes, insects and amphibians. Recent additions to the buildings include the novel aviary designed by Lord Snowdon and Sir Hugh Casson's elephant house. Conducted boat trips are available on the Regent's canal which runs along the northern flank of the Zoo and into the popular and colourful Little Venice, a yachting basin full of small boats.

Grosvenor Square is named after Sir Richard Grosvenor, a wealthy landowner, who developed the site towards the end of the eighteenth century. One of the oldest of London's squares, it is dominated today by the modern-style American Embassy which takes up the whole of the west side. Known as "Little America" since the Second World War though its American associations go back much earlier to 1785 when John Adams, later to become the second President of the United States, lived at No. 9 in capacity of ambassador. In the public gardens there is a bronze statue of President F.D. Roosevelt which was unveiled by his widow in the presence of King George VI and Queen Elizabeth in 1948.

Leicester Square, surrounded by cinemas and restaurants takes its name from the second Earl of Leicester who had a house on the north side in 1631. The present square dates from 1874 when it was laid out by Albert Grant who also provided the central white marble fountain and statue of Shakespeare.

Piccadilly Circus at night is a blaze of colour from the huge animated neon advertisements. Situated at the centre of London's entertainment world in the West End it is a great attraction to tourists who are drawn to it by some mysterious force — perhaps by the statue of Eros affectionately thought of as the god of love, but in reality an aluminium portrayal of the Angel of Christian Charity, erected in 1893 as a tribute to that great Victorian philanthropist, the Earl of Shaftesbury.

Trafalgar Square commemorating Nelson's naval victory of 1805, was designed by Sir Charles Barry, and laid out between 1829 and 1841. Commanding the square is Nelson's column, a fluted granite shaft nearly 185 feet high topped by another 17 feet of E.H. Baily's statue of England's greatest naval hero. The four bronze lions at the column's base are the work of Sir Edwin Landseer and were not placed until 1868, some 26 years after the column was erected.

The fountains and friendly pigeons make Trafalgar Square a popular rendezvous for Londoner and tourist alike, whilst its sheer size and central position provides a focal point for political demonstrations and public meetings.

Grosvenor Square: President F.D. Roosevelt.

Grosvenor Square: the American Embassy.

Prospects of Piccadilly Circus: the once-called "hub of the Empire".

Trafalgar Square, the true heart of London. ▷

PICCADILLY CIRCUS W1

CITY OF WESTMINSTER

Concorde taking off from Heathrow (London's airport).

Welcome to Heathrow Airport

GETTING ABOUT

An increasing number of London's visitors arrive by air at Heathrow, one of the world's busiest international airports, now conveniently connected to the capital by means of the Piccadilly Line.

The best way of exploring London is as a pedestrian roaming from any one of a dozen centres, but for the longer journey a wide choice of London's red buses is available, as well as the equally famous black taxis, both an established part of the London scene. The Underground (much of it *above* ground in fact, though *not* overhead) serves the whole metropolis and has the added atraction of being free from road traffic jams. The Circle line offers a two-way route conveniently enabling the visitor to reach many places of interest. London Transport run regular sightseeing bus tours and conducted coach tours to the more popular tourist attractions in and around London and issue excellent descriptive guide books, leaflets, and maps.

Travel: overground and Underground.

Fortnum and Mason (top), *Burlington Arcade* (bottom), and (right) *Carnaby Street.*

Harrods, shopping mecca of the world.

SHOPPING, EATING AND ENTERTAINMENT

Serious shopping or just browsing are equally rewarding experiences in London whose range of shops, stores, and stalls cater for all tastes — and purses. Carnaby Street achieved fame overnight in the late 1960's when it became the mecca of ultra-modern fashion and its influence rapidly spread throughout the capital, and indeed the world, as evidenced by the now common-place boutiques specialising in clothes for young people. *Haute couture*, exclusive and expensive, is to be found in and

Marks & Spencer, Marble Arch.

Selfridges, Oxford Street.

Foyles, Charing Cross Road.   Hatchards, Piccadilly.

around fashionable Mayfair and Knightsbridge, whilst in-between tastes are well served by the Marks & Spencer stores, justifiably well-known for their consistently good value in an increasingly wide range of goods. Regent Street, New Bond Street, and Burlington Arcade offer the best in expensive jewellery, as does Jermyn Street in mens' wear.

Shopping in the exclusive Harrods store in Knightsbridge is not necessarily expensive and its ability to supply every possible demand — well almost — has made it legendary. Oxford Street is all shops with a preponderance selling nothing but footwear and is also the home of several departmental stores including Selfridge's, Debenhams, D.H. Evans, John Lewis, and C & A.

Old and new books are a speciality of Hatchards in Picca-dilly and others are in Charing Cross Road led by Foyles ("the biggest bookshop in the world"). Art dealers of all kinds abound in St. James's, Knightsbridge, and Bond Street, and the auction rooms of Sotheby's, Christie's, and others offer excitement and interest.

Not to be missed are the colourful street markets (there are nearly 100 of them in London) where the entertain-ment is free and bargains abound. A very pleasant Sunday morning can be spent just wandering around Petticoat Lane (Middlesex Street) in London's East End and the neighbouring Club Row (Sclater Street) where children especially will be enthralled by the animals on sale —all kinds, shapes and sizes. Leather Lane (Holborn) is a weekday general market where household goods, fruit and vegetables are sold or if we believe the stallholders, given away! The antique bargain hunter should try his luck in Portobello Road, W10 or Camden Passage, Isling-ton where the speciality is antiques — mostly old and genuine but with the inevitable sprinkling of the repro-duction.

A sale in progress at Christie's.

The many faces and facets of London's famous Portobello Road Antiques Market.

The public house: an essential part of English life and the London Scene.

In the heart of the City, Leadenhall market, originally sold poultry but now also offers a variety of groceries and greengroceries.

You have to be an early riser to see the meat market at Smithfield or Billingsgate fish market in action. Both are essentially wholesale but there is a certain amount of retail business in the surrounding areas. The vegetable, fruit and flower market centred on Covent Garden for hundreds of years now has a new home at Nine Elms on the South Bank. The old site, largely derelict, is patiently awaiting redevelopment.

When it comes to eating the choice is endless. The ubiquitous sandwich is available at numerous coffee-bars or from that great British establishment, the pub, which can take the form of the chromium plated ultra-modern to the red plush and mirrored old tavern, or a peculiar compromise of the two. Light refreshments can be had at most pubs and many have excellent restaurants. Beer, that uniquely English drink, be it the sharp tasting pale golden bitter or the sweeter dark brown ale goes down well with a ploughman's lunch (crusty bread, butter, cheese and pickles).

Specialities of London's East End are the nearly instant and very nutritious fish and chips, and a wide range of sea foods (jellied eels, whelks, cockles, shrimps, crab, lobster and mussels) still sold from roadside stalls. All the large department stores have restaurant facilities and a choice of international cuisine is available from a multitude of hotels and restaurants in the West End.

London's theatres: Coliseum (left) *and Theatre Royal* (bottom).

Characteristic Soho by night

The Windmill (bottom).

"When one is tired of London, one is tired of life; for there is in London all that life can afford." Quite possibly not in the context intended but Doctor Johnson's words are very apposite to the tremendous variety of entertainment available; theatres, cinemas, discotheques, gambling (legalised now), the racy strip-clubs of Soho, music concerts on the South Bank, at the Wigmore Hall, the Royal Albert Hall or in the summer months by the lake in the open-air at Kenwood. Ballet and opera at the Coliseum and Covent Garden. For the sporting enthusiast there is a choice of football, tennis, ice-skating, fishing, boating, sailing, swimming, bowling (indoor and outdoor), skiing on artificial slopes, greyhound racing, and riding.

London policemen are always at hand to assist the visitor.

The passing scene. ▷

London characters: Pearly Kings and Queens (top),
and Flower Lady (bottom).

Hot chestnut vendor (top), *and a rare sight these days,
a chimney sweep* (bottom).

The passing scene.

Patriotic to the end!

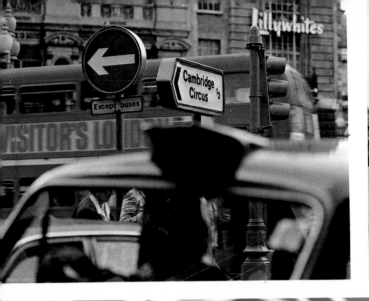

Contents

ACKNOWLEDGMENTS:

The arms of the City of London, Greater London Council and the City of Westminster, on the title page and cover, are reproduced by kind permission of the appropriate authority.

The publishers gratefully acknowledge photographic facilities made available by the administrators of St. Paul's Cathedral, Westminster Abbey, the Spanish and Portuguese Synagogue, St. Bartholomew the Great, Westminster Cathedral, W. & G. Foyle Ltd., Harrods Ltd., and Marks & Spencer Ltd.

The photographs in this book were taken specially by the staff photographer of FISA Industrias Gráficas with the exception of the following, which appear by arrangement with: The Trustees of the British Museum. The Museum of London. The Corporation of London Records Office. A.F. Kersting. Eric Restall. Crown copyright reserved and reproduced by permission of the Controller of Her Majesty's Stationery Office. Tom Hanley. Colour Library International. Lloyds of London. The Stock Exchange. The Royal Society. National Maritime Museum. Mike Roberts. The Tate Gallery. The Royal Academy of Arts. The Trustees of the National Gallery. Courtauld Institute Galleries. The Governors of Dulwich College Picture Gallery. Christie's. Trustees of Sir John Soane's Museum. The Greater London Council as Trustees of the Iveagh Bequest, Kenwood. Victoria & Albert Museum, Crown copyright. Trustees of the British Museum (Natural History). Institute of Geological Sciences. Science Museum. Madame Tussaud's, interior photographs. Trustees of the Wallace Collection. The Lord Chamberlain's office: Crown copyright reserved. British Airways. British Airports Authority. British Tourist Authority and Department of the Environment.

The printing of this book was completed in the workshops of FISA - Industrias Gráficas, Palaudarias, 26 - Barcelona (Spain)